THE BASICS OF ELECTRONICS

DAVID ASKEW

Copyright © 2024 by David Askew

All rights reserved. This book or any of its portion may not be reproduced or transmitted in any means, electronic or mechanical, including recording, photocopying, or by any information storage and retrieval system, without the prior written permission of the copyright holder except in the case of brief quotations embodied in critical reviews and other noncommercial uses permitted by copyright law.

Printed in the United States of America
Library of Congress Control Number: 2024924952
ISBN: Softcover   979-8-89518-570-4
        Hardback   979-8-89518-694-7
        e-Book   979-8-89518-571-1
Published by: WP Lighthouse
Publication Date: 12/12/2024

To buy a copy of this book, please contact:
WP Lighthouse
Phone: +1-888-668-2459
support@wplighthouse.com
wplighthouse.com

This book was not intended for Electrical Engineers, but trades people and hobbyists

This book does not get into sophisticated theories of electronics, but basic everyday use of electronics. There will be some references to the fact that other characteristics are involved and require more sophisticated formulas than shown.

The reason for writing this book is that I work in the electronics trades industry. However, several of the technicians do not understand the basics of electronics. Also, I know several hobbyists that want to learn about electronics.

This book includes experiments, lists of suggested suppliers, and other reference material.

At the back there is an appendix that includes the suggested vendor list, suggested test equipment, and reference material.

My education includes an associate's degree in electrical engineering, from SUNY at Morrisville, New York. My father was in electronics, so he got me started when I was 9 years old. In my earlier years I worked in a TV shop. I then went In the Air Force and had additional training on broadcast equipment. When I left the Air Force, I got a job with a company that designed and installed TV studios, media systems, CCTV and sound systems. After 20 years, I changed jobs to a company that did CCTV, card access, security systems, fire, nurse call, media systems, and sound systems. With both companies I did system design, programming, and testing. I was sent to many manufacturers' schools for additional training. As well I have built wired and wireless remote-control systems and was a mentor with the local high school's robotics program in the 1990's. Thus, I have had a lot of hands-on experience.

Contents

Chapter 1 : Basic Electronics 1

Chapter 2 : Meters and Standard Material...2

Chapter 3 : DC Theory 7

Chapter 4 : Resistors 9

Chapter 5 : Oscilloscope 17

Chapter 6 : AC Theory 20

Chapter 7 : Capacitors 22

Chapter 8 : Inductors and Transformers 27

Chapter 9 : Other Signals 33

Chapter 10 : Diodes 35

Chapter 11 : Switches 39

Chapter 12 : Relays and Solenoids 41

Chapter 13 : Transistors 44

Chapter 14 : Audio 46

Chapter 15 : Trouble Shooting 51

Appendix 53

Chapter 1
Basic Electronics

As I said in my intro, I am not going to go into deep electronics theory.

Electronics consist of Protons, a positive charge, Electrons, a negative charge, and Neutrons, which are neutral.

Electronics theory says that electrons flow, however most electronic symbols show the flow going from positive to negative. Therefore, this book will be based on Proton or Positive Voltage Flow. The following picture shows the positive side of the battery connected to the anode side of a diode and following the arrow to the cathode.

Figure 1

Electronics uses two types of voltage Direct Current known as DC and Alternating Current known as AC. Other signals used in electronics are RF radio frequency and Serial which consists of digital signals in a sequence.

Electronics use several components. The following is just a list of a few of them. We will discuss most of these products in further chapters.

Resistor, capacitors, Diodes, coils, transformers, transistors, IC's, batteries, LED's, LCD display, switches, buttons, and connectors.

Chapter 2
Meters and Standard Material

I am including this chapter because meters are used in several of the labs. There are several types of meters, as shown in figure 3. In the appendix are lists of vendors that can supply meters.

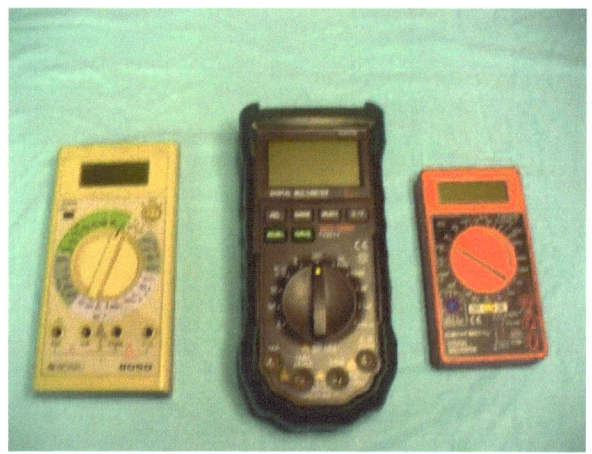

Figure2

Let's first talk about the common features of meters. As different style meters can include a lot of different measurements.

Volts: All meters have AC and DC voltage scales.

Amps: All meters have AC and DC amp scales.

Ohms: All meters include a resistance scale known as ohms.

Other features found in some meters, capacitance test, diode test, continuity, transistor testing, inductance, DB decibels, and frequency.

One of the most important factors when using a meter is to plug the test lead in the correct connectors. Use the owner's manual for this information.

Some meters are auto scaling and some are manual select.

Manual select meters require setting the voltage, current or ohms based on a range from 0 to the highest value on the selector.

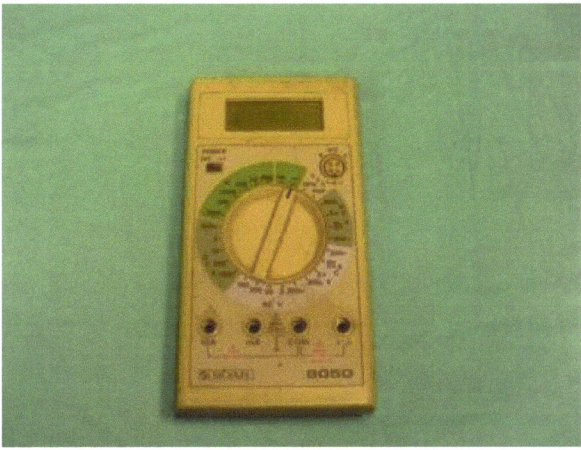

Figure 3

In figure 3, this meter has DC voltage scales of 2, 20, 200, and 1000 volts. The ohms scale has 200, 2k, 20k, 200k, 2m, and 20m. The current scales are 200 ma, 20ma/10A this is determined by which input terminal is being used, 2 ma and 200 μa.

Most meters require selecting AC or DC, either by the dial, or by a push button selection. Read the owner's manual for proper operation.

Auto scaling meters only require selecting the right format such as voltage, current, or ohms. These meters will require selecting AC or DC typically through a push button and then they go the full voltage or current or ohms range of the meter automatically. In figure 4, volts only have one setting, however current has 3 settings.

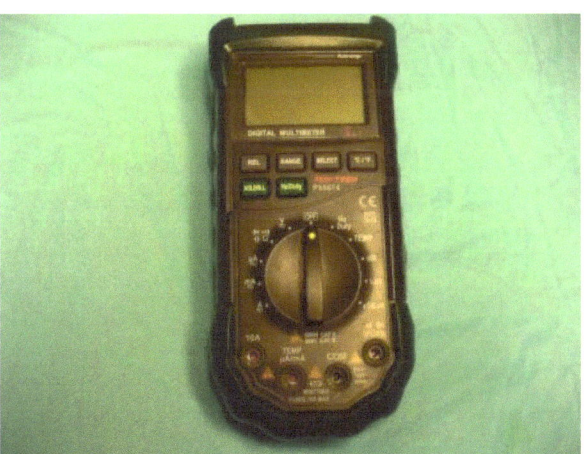

Figure 4

Meters have several connection terminals. Be sure to connect to the correct plug-in terminal and set for the function being used. Let's discuss the different terminal inputs on the meter shown in figure 5. The far-right terminal is for the positive lead when measuring volts, ohms, capacitance, frequency, and diode test. The next terminal on the right is the common terminal. This terminal is used as the negative terminal with volts, ohms, capacitance frequency, diode test, low current, and temperature. The next terminal on the right is used for low current and temperature. The far-left terminal is used for high current up to 10 amps.

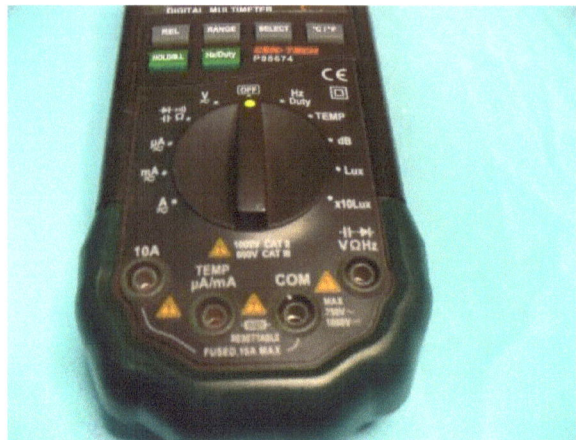

Figure 5

Some additional features of meters require using push buttons for sub selection. For example, one of my meters when using the ohms scale you can push a button to select diode mode or a continuity sounder.

An accessory I highly recommend is a test lead set with clips. Some meters, however, come with clips that slip over the end of the test lead. In the appendix is a list of vendors that can supply this material. Most meters come standard with probes only, but you will find it is hard to hold both probes on a circuit at the same time. Therefore, the clips come in handy to make a connection to circuit.

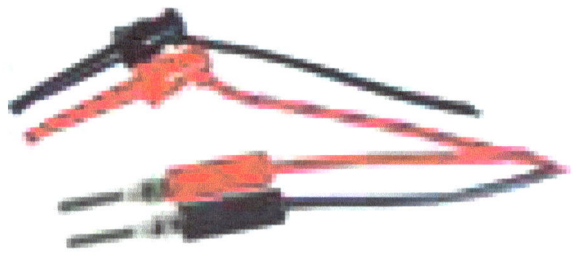

Figure 6

Standard Material Recommended for Labs

The following lists either basic assemble your own lab unit or purchase a factory-built lab unit.

To basic build your own lab, use the following parts.

Test punch block and wire jumpers. You can buy kits of precut jumpers, or you can buy 20 gauge solid wire to make jumpers.

The following is a kit of a perf board with wire jumpers. In the appendix is a list of vendors that can supply this material.

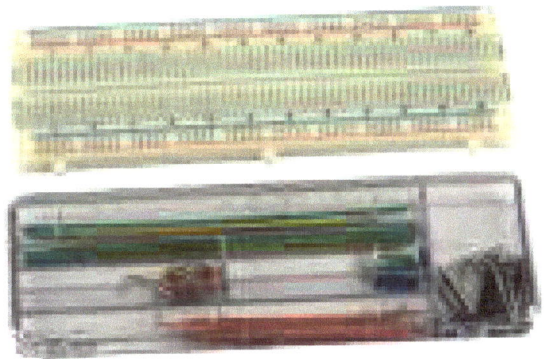

Figure 7

Power Supply:

Some lab test units come complete with built-in power supplies. You can purchase variable power supplies that can be set to 12 or 5 volts. These will be the most common voltages we will work with in the labs. Information on these power supplies can be found in the appendix.

Already manufactured lab unit:

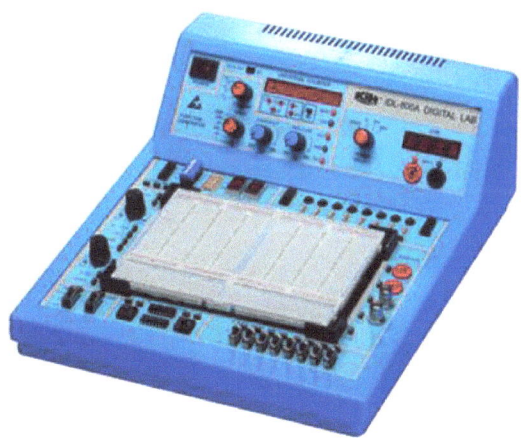

Figure 8

Or you can build your own unit as I did with many common functions I use.

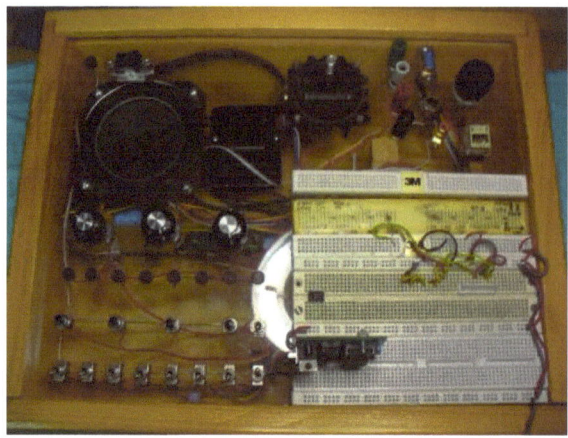

Figure 9

Another device needed in some of the labs will be a test signal generator. Note that some of the pre-made lab units have signal generators built in. You can purchase a scope unit that connects to a computer. These units typically have test generators built in. In the appendix is a list of vendors that supply test generators.

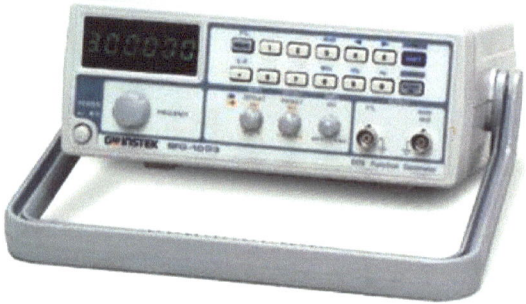

Figure 10

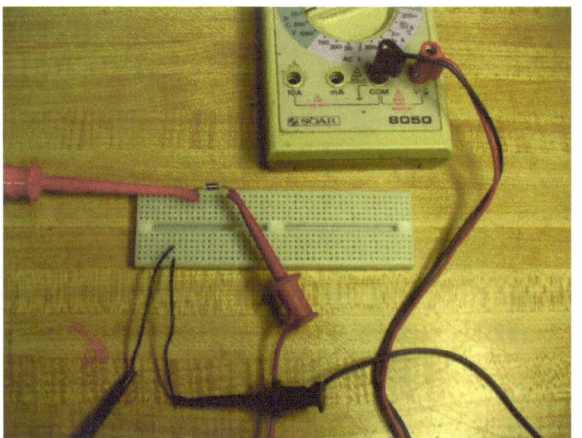

Figure This is an example of wiring using a perf test board. The leads coming from the left are from the power supply and the leads going to the right go to the meter. Push the leads of the components into the holes on the perf board. The columns from top to bottom are connected together. The large space in the center of the board going left to right divides the columns so the bottom set of columns are separate from the top set of columns. As you can see the two black wires are in the same column connecting these two negatives together. Typically, red is used for positive and black is used for negative.

Chapter 3
DC Theory

When talking about DC we will talk about Voltage measured in Volts, Current, measured in Amps, Resistance, measured in Ohms, and Power measured in Watts.

DC power sources can be batteries, power supplies that convert AC outlet power to DC, generators and solar panels.

DC voltage has one direction of voltage flowing at a time. Figure 11 shows the positive side of the power source flowing through the diode. These devices will be talked about in later chapters.

Figure 11

Lab 1

Take a 12 volt power source and connect the positive end to the anode side of the diode. Secondly connect the positive lead of the meter to the cathode side of the diode. Lastly, connect the negative lead of the meter to the negative side of the power supply. As shown in figure 12. In the appendix is a list of vendors that can supply this material.

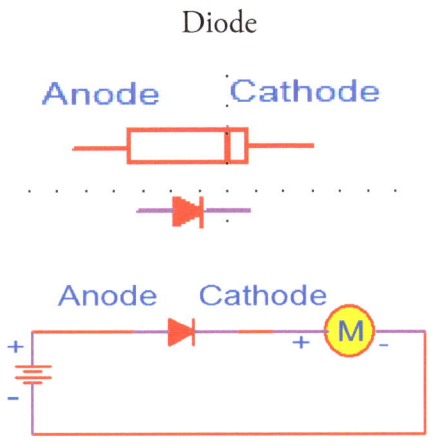

Figure 12

Select DC voltage on the meter. Make note the voltage reading_____

Lab 2

Now let's reverse the diode as shown in figure 13. Connect the positive side of the power source to the cathode lead of the diode. Then connect the anode side of the diode to the meter plus lead. Lastly, connect the negative meter lead to the negative side of the power source.

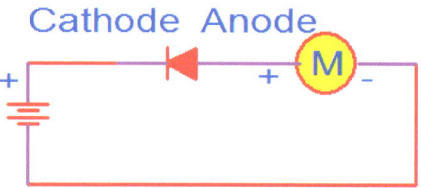

Figure 13

Select DC voltage on the meter. Make note the voltage reading_____

You should get a zero-voltage reading. This shows how important polarity is with DC voltage.

Answers to questions

Lab1   Should be about 11.3 VDC

Lab2   Should be 0 VDC

Chapter 4
Resistors

The next chapter is about resistors. DC voltage and current can be controlled through resistors. Resistance is really important both in electronic circuit components and in wire. As wires have resistance to them. Resistors are used for voltage drop, current reduction, and end of line termination. In the appendix you will find a chart with wire size and resistance values.

As the word Resistance consists of Resist, Resistors create Voltage and current drops.

Let's work with resistor formulas known as Ohms Law. Later we will get into lab projects showing the results from your formulas.

The symbol for a fixed resistor is ⌁, symbol for a variable resistor ⌁

Resistors come in many shapes and sizes. Shapes can be tubular, rectangular or surface mounted and variable resistors typically have a round base with a shaft.

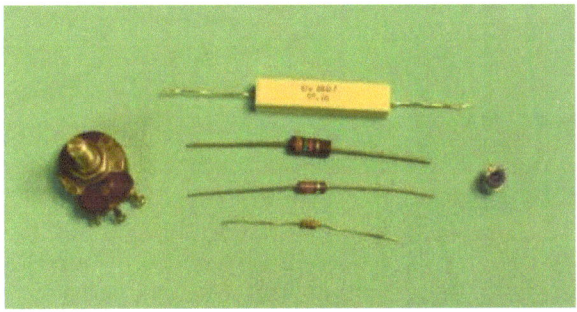

Figure 14

The following are the different Ohms Law Formulas

(R) Stands for Ohms

(E) Stands for Volts

(I) Stands for Amps

(P) Stands for Watts

1K = 1,000

1M = 1,000,000

I=E/R is used to calculate current when you know the voltage and resistance.

E=I*R is used to calculate voltage when you know the current and resistance

R=E/I is used to calculate resistance when you know voltage and current.

P=I*E is used to calculate power when you know the voltage and current.

Note there are other variances of these formulas. For example, if you want to calculate power but you only know the voltage and resistance. Use this formula.

P=E*E/R

A handy tool is the resistor color code chart.

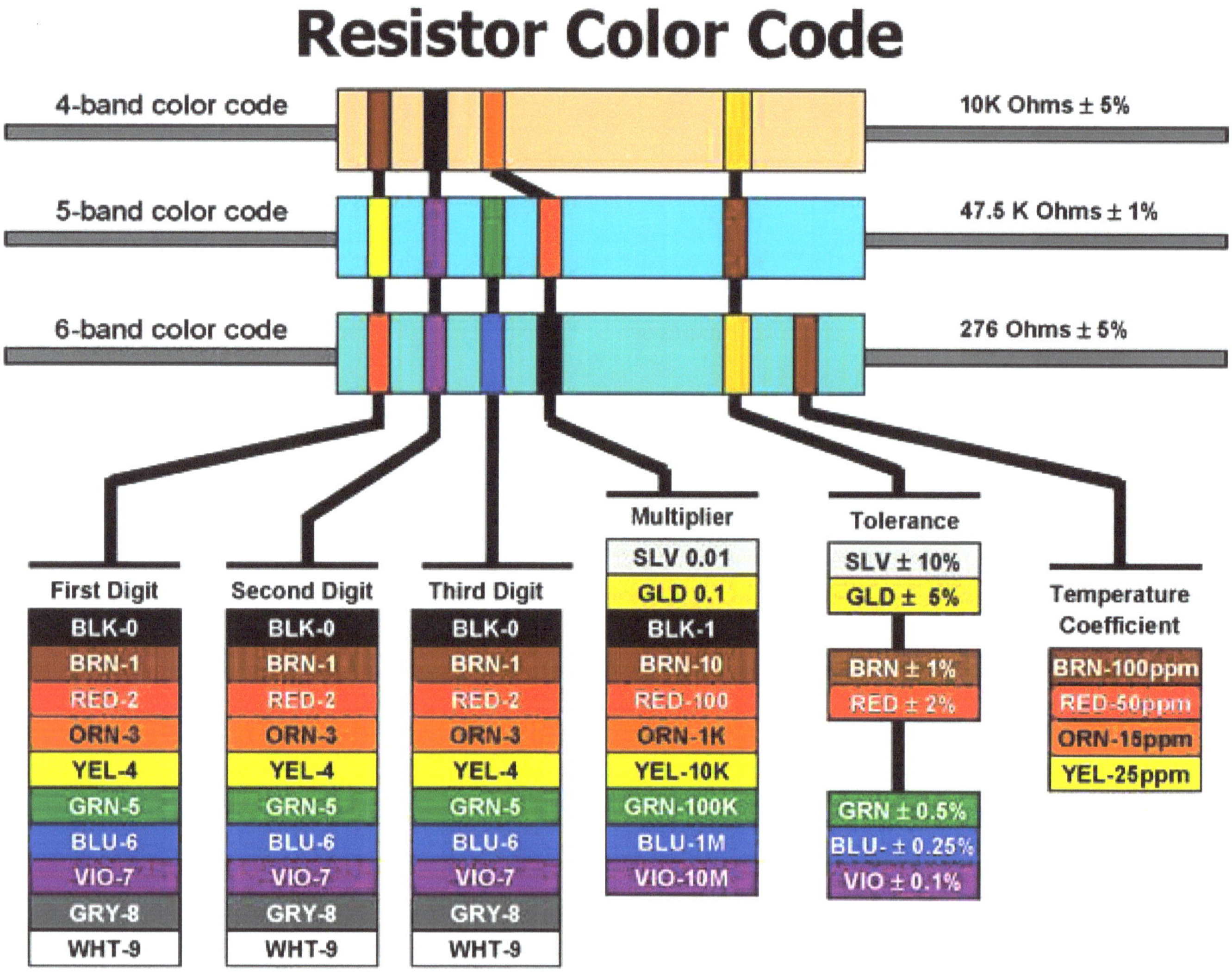

Figure 15

Calculating series resistor circuits. You take R1 + R2= total resistance. For addition resistors continue adding them together.

The formula for calculating current in a series circuit you use the following formula. I=E/R. Note in a series circuit the current will be the same through all resistors.

Now to calculate the individual voltage across each resistor you use the formula E=I*R. So, you take the current figured in the above formula and multiply it times each individual resistor.

In the next lab we will use a 1000-ohm resistor as R1. The colors for this resistor are Brown, Black and Red, for the 2200-ohm resistor they are Red, Red, and Red, as R2. Note we are using the 4-band color code. Band 1 is the 1st value, band 2 is the 2nd value, and band 3 is the 3rd value and the 4 band is multiplier in 10's.

Lab 3

Reference Figure 16

Let's take a 12-volt power source connect the positive side of the power source to one end of the 1000 ohm resistor, then tie the other end of the 1000 ohm and one end of the 2200 ohm resistors together, then tie the other side of the 2200 ohm resistor to the negative side of the power supply. Now take the positive lead of your meter to the tie point of the two resistors and connect the negative lead to the negative side of the power supply. Measure the voltage between the negative side of the power and the center point of the resistors. This value should be close to value calculated in the above formula. Note these values will not be exactly the same as your calculation, because most resistors have tolerance between 5 and 10 percent.

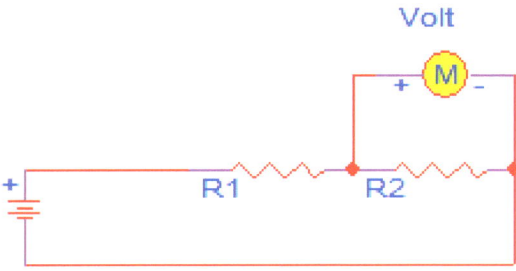

Figure 16

Note when doing any lab assignment be sure the power source is off while making connections.

Now let's calculate the current flowing through the two resistors. Note when resistors are in series the current will be the same through both resistors. Use the following formula

I = E/R now take the real values and insert them in the formula.

Question 5: I = 12/3200 what is the result._____

Lab 4

Now for a lab assignment, take and disconnect the positive side of the 12 volts and connect to the positive lead of you meter, be sure to use the right connection on your meter for current. Then tie the negative lead of the meter to R1. Connect R1 and R2 in series as shown in figure 17. Then tie the other end of R2 to the negative side of the power supply. Be sure your meter is set to DC current, if not you can damage your meter. Note you should get a reading similar to you calculation. Note these values will not be the same as your calculation because most resistors have tolerance between 5 and 10 percent.

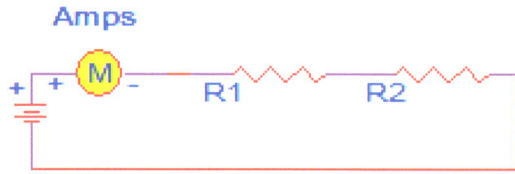

Figure 17

Note when doing any lab assignment be sure the power source is off while making connections.

Now let's talk about parallel resistors. The formula for parallel resistors is

R total = 1/ (1/R1 + 1/R2)

Question 6: Now let's apply real resistor values, we will use the 1K as R1 and 2.2K as R2 values. Used in the last lab and parallel them using the formula R total = 1/ (1/R1 +1/ R2) what is the total resistance _____

Now let's calculate the total current through the circuit. Use formula I = E/R and use the resistance value calculated in question 6.

Question 7: Value. _____

Now let's calculate the current through each resistor. Use the formula I = E/R. Since the resistors are paralleled, the voltage is the same across both resistors.

Question 8: Now using this formula calculate the current through R1._____

Question 9: Then using the formula again calculate the current through R2._____

Lab 5

Lab Connect one end of both resistors together then connect to the positive side of the power. Now connect the meter in series like we did in the previous lab through each resistor. Remove the meter from R1, connect the

R1 resistor lead to the negative side of the power supply. Now move R2 from the negative side of the power and connect to the positive lead of the meter.

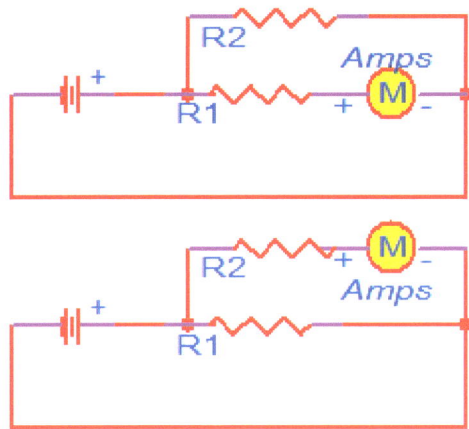

Figure 18

Note when doing any lab assignment be sure the power source is off while making connections.

Current for R1_____ You will need to set your meter to the mA scale. This should be close to the figure calculated in question 8.

Current for R2_____ You will need to set your meter to the mA scale. This should be close to the figure calculated in question 9.

Lab 6

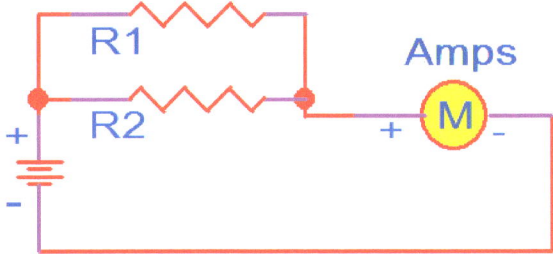

Now tie both of the ends of the resistors that were separate together and tie the current meter in series. What current, reading do you get. _____ This should be close to the figure calculated in question 7.

Wire resistance Note I am not listing any lab on this topic because of shock and fire danger.

Wire has resistance and becomes important on length, based on the amount of current draw. Example are, power extension cords, and what you can plug in the end of the cord and what gauge wire the cord has.

Let's take a 100ft 18-gauge extension cord. The resistance of 18-gauge wire is .0062 ohms per Ft. All power cords consist of 2 conductors, and some have a third conductor, one called line or the hot lead, and one called neutral or the return lead. A third lead is called neutral or gnd. The formula would be 100 for the length, times .0062 ohms per foot. So, the total resistance for the 100ft extension cord 100 * .0062 this is .62 ohms. Let's start with a hedge trimmer, these typically draw 3.8 amps, let's use the ohms law formula E=I*R. Where E equals volt, I equal amps and R equals ohms. E=3.8*.62 the result is approximately 2.356 volts drop. The hedge trimmer should work properly. However, if you were to use a 200ft extension the voltage drop will be equal to 5.55 voltage drop, this may be a problem. Now let's change our cable to 16-gauge wire. Using the same formulas, we used above. The 16-gauge wire has a .0042 ohms per foot and multiplying 100 ft. we get .42 ohms. Using the same formulas we did above. E = IR, E equals the same 3.8 amps we did above times .42 ohms equals, 1.596 VAC. Now we take 120VAC – 1.596 equals 118VAC, the hedge trimmer should work with this voltage loss.

Note I am not doing a lab on this because it is too dangerous to deal with 120 VAC if you are not certified to do this.

The following is an example's that would relate to the technology field.

An example involving a fire alarm signaling circuit with several signaling devices, may have too much voltage drop for the last device on the circuit to work properly, or a paging system having too many speakers and the speakers at the end of the line may be very week.

Let's calculate the loss for the fire alarm signaling circuit. A typical fire alarm Audio Visual device used as a strobe and sounder on a fire system draws .188 amps each. These devices are connected in parallel. Now let's say you have a long hall that will require 40 of these devices, and you start out using 16-gauge wire. Now take .188 amps time 40 devices you get 7.52 amps, and let's say the cable run from the fire panel to the last device is 300ft. As we discussed earlier, 16-gauge wire is .004 ohms per ft. with the cable consisting of two conductors. We will multiply 300 * .004 we get 1.2 ohms. Now let's calculate the voltage loss. E=I * R, 7.52 amps times 1.2 ohms we get 9.02-volt loss. Most fire alarm devices are 24 volts DC, so if we subtract 9.02 volts from 24 volts, we get 14.97 volts. The specific device I picked has a minimal operating voltage, of 16 volts, so the devices towards the end of the run would not work properly. Now let's redo our design and use 14-gauge wires with a loss of .0026 ohms per ft. With 300 ft. times * .0026 = .78 ohms: Now with the Current of 7.52 time .78 ohms we get a voltage drop of 5.86. Now we subtract this from 24 volts we get 18.13 volts so the last device will be within the 16 volt limit.

Another application of resistors is for end of line termination. This is done in fire alarm systems, broadband TV, Security systems, and many more applications. If you have the wrong end of line value, you may get trouble on the fire alarm system, and for TV you will end up with either ghosting, or noise in the image.

Let's talk about power. Power is important with resistors and many other devices. Power will determine the size of the device. As I mentioned at the beginning of this chapter resistors come in many shapes and sizes, one of the factors is the power rating of resistors is in watts.

Let's use formula P = I * E. Use the following figure to calculate both the voltage and current readings. Note the meter is shown in two parts of the diagram, in the lab you will take the voltage measurement 1st, and then move the meter to take the current reading, note you will need to change the meter setting from volts to amps.

Note when doing any lab assignment be sure the power source is off while making connections.

Using this diagram figure 23 assemble your circuit, but only use the meter in the 1st step to measure voltage, Then shut power down, move the meter to the current position. R1 will be the 1,000 ohm resistor and the power source should be 12 volts.

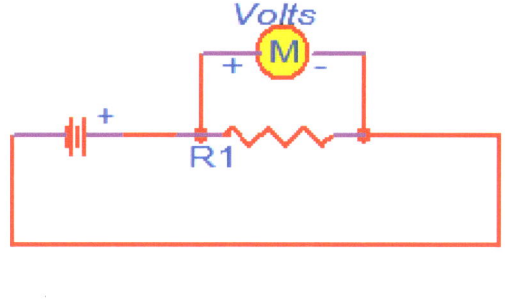

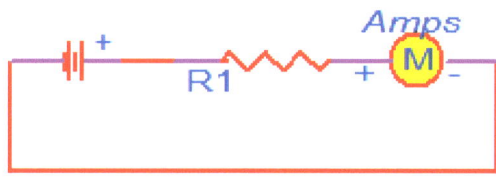

Figure 23

Question 10: Voltage reading_____

Question 11: Current reading_____

Question 12: Now using the P=I*E formula, calculate the power. This is important to determine the wattage value of the resistor. _____

When designing circuits, you always want your actual part power value to be at least 25% higher than the circuit power. So, with the above wattage value, add 25% to it to determine the value you should at least have. To add this 25% use P*1.25.

Question 13: So, the value you end up with is _____

Resistors typically come in 1/8, 1/4, 1/2, 1, 2, 5 and many other wattage sizes. If you use to lower wattage resistor than the design above will burn up.

Answers to questions

Question 1: 3.2 K or 3200 ohms

Question 2: .3125

Question 3: 3.744 VDC

Question 4: 8.256 VDC

Question 5: 3.75 mA or .00375 amps.

Question 6: 687.3 Ohms, note I rounded the figure.

Question 7: 17.5 mA or .0175 amps, note I rounded the figure

Question 8: 12 mA or .012 amps.

Question 9: 5.5 mA or .0055 amps, note I rounded the figure

Question 10: 12 VDC

Question 11: 12 mA or .012 amps.

Question 12: .144 watts

Question 13: .18 watts

Chapter 5
Oscilloscope

Oscilloscopes are used to measure AC, DC and several types of wave shapes.

Oscilloscopes come in many shapes and sizes, and now available are computer oscilloscope interfaces. In the appendix is a list of vendors that can supply oscilloscopes.

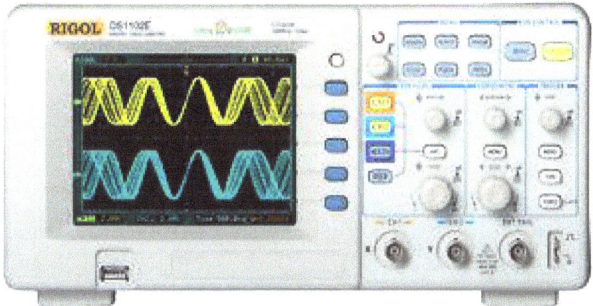

Figure 19

Standard Oscilloscope

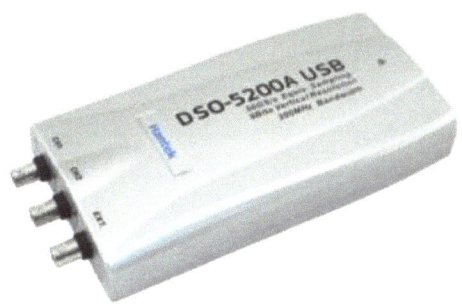

Figure 20

Computer oscilloscope interface

Scope probes are pretty much standard, with a ground clip and a probe that can clip to a circuit, or the clip probe comes off leaving a pointed tip to use. Some probes have built in attenuators of 10X or 100X for larger voltage use.

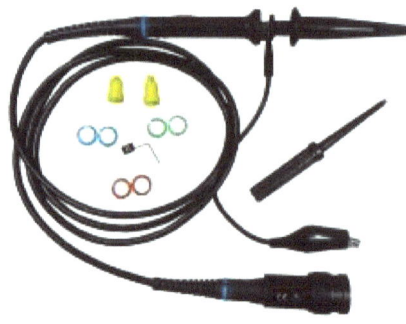

Figure 21

Now let's do a lab that will show the shape of DC voltage.

Lab 7

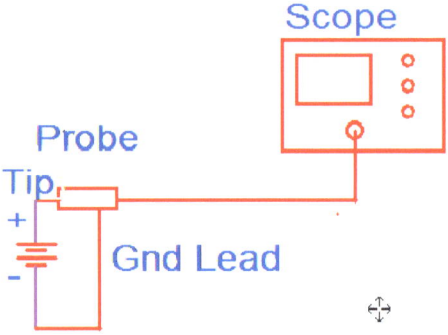

The symbol on the left is a battery symbol, and the battery uses in this project is 12VDC, note you can also use a 12VDC power supply.

Read the instruction manual with the scope or computer scope module on how to set the volts per division/CH-1 input level and vertical position. Also read how to set the Horizontal/sweep time per division.

Take your oscilloscope or scope probe tied to a computer. Set the volts/division or CH-1 to read 5 or 10 volts per unit. Set the sweep time/division or Horizontal to 1 millisecond. Set the vertical position so the Line is in the center of the screen. Now connect the probe tip to the plus side of the power and the negative or scope ground lead to the negative side of the power. Set your scope to DC input. You will have a straight line. The line with zero is 0 volts DC reference, this is where the line was before connecting to the power note the new line is above the center line indicating 12VDC.

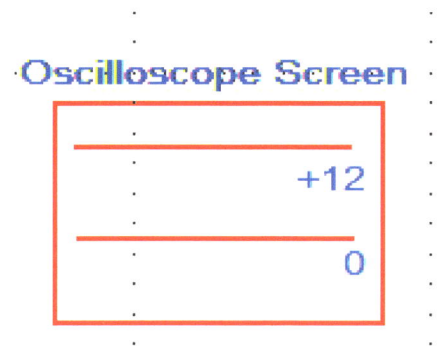

Figure 22

Note when doing any lab assignment be sure the power source is off while making connections.

Chapter 6
AC Theory

As the word alternate indicates the voltage is not a straight line. Examples of AC voltage are sound, Video, test generators, motors, TV, Radio signals, and many more systems.

AC signal can come in many shapes including sine waves 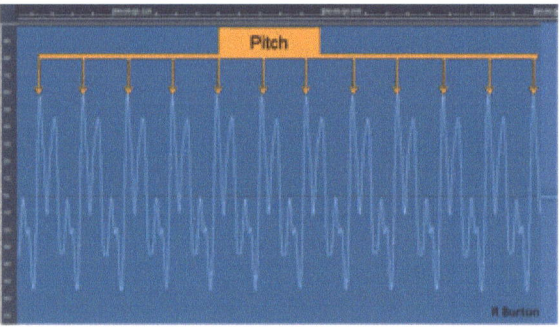 this shape is a perfect sine wave however an audio signal will be several different shapes. Other common shapes are saw tooth and square waves.

Figure 24

Example of an Audio signal: Audio signals can vary in many ways depending on the particular notes being played.

With AC we talk about voltage, current, impedance and frequency.

Note when doing any lab assignment be sure the power source is off while making connections.

In the appendix is a list of vendors that can supply the material and test equipment

Lab 8

Take your oscilloscope or scope probe tied to a computer. Set the volts/division or CH-1 to read 1 or 5 volts per unit. Set the sweep time/division or Horizontal to 250 microseconds. Set the vertical position so the Line is in the center of the screen. Now connect the probe tip to the plus side of the function generator and the negative or scope ground lead to the negative side of the function generator. Set your scope to AC input. Set the function generator to 1,000 Hz. Note there are other settings needed in the oscilloscope, such as trigger. See the manual for further detail.

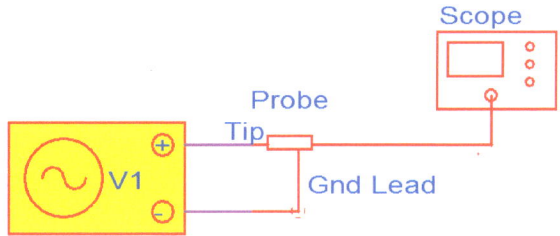

Figure 28

Note the shape. It should look like the following

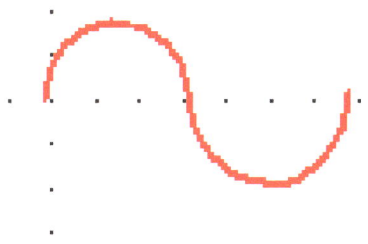

Figure 26

Sound is a form of AC voltage. In the last chapter we talked about resistors and voltage and current, the same goes for AC voltage and resistors.

Chapter 7
Capacitors

Capacitors have several different characteristics. With capacitors we talk about capacity value which is measured in Farad. However, a 1 Farad capacitor is very large so most capacitors are measured in Micro farad. With the symbol, UF. 1/1,000,000 or .000001. Capacitors come in many shapes and sizes.

Figure 27

The parameters we talk about with capacitors are:

Capacitance shown as C

Frequency shown as F

Voltage shown as V

Impedance is shown in Ohms Ω. Impedance is the AC version of resistance.

Polarity, this is important when using electrolytic capacitors because they are polarized.

Let's talk about what capacitors do.

Capacitors pass AC signals based on the capacitor value and the frequencies being used, and block DC voltage.

Capacitors are used to also to filter power supplies.

Depending on the value of the capacitor will determine what frequencies the capacitor will pass. The larger the capacitor value the lower frequencies pass and the lower the capacity value only higher frequencies are passed.

Capacitors can also build up a charge, so when disconnecting a capacitor from a live circuit, you may want to use a jumper across the leads to discharge the capacitor.

The formula for figuring impedance is XC = 1/(2*π*F*C). Let's apply this. The frequency will be 60 Hertz, the capacity will be 1000 μF (.001 Farad). π Note this is Pi equal to 3.14

Question 1: What will the impedance be. _____

Now let's change the capacity value to 1 μF (.000001 Farad).

Question 2: what will the impedance be. _____

Lab 9

We will be using a 1,000 μF electrolytic capacitor. Electrolytic capacitors are polarity sensitive. Figure 28A shows the symbol for An Electrolytic capacitor. Note white area with dashes, this is the negative lead of the electrolytic capacitor. See figure 28B

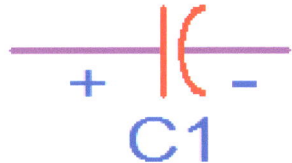

Figure 28A

Figure 28B

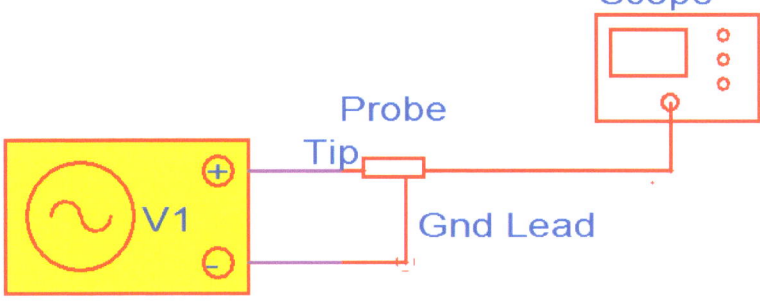

Figure 29A

Hook up the circuit shown in figure 29A. Now take the scope probe tip and connect to the generator positive output and the negative scope lead to the generator ground.

On the Scope set the volts/division or CH-1 to read 1 or 5 volts per unit. Set the sweep time/division or Horizontal to 250 microseconds. Set the vertical position so the Line is in the center of the screen. Now connect the probe tip to the plus side of the function generator and the negative or scope ground lead to the negative side of the function generator. Set your scope to AC input. Set the function generator to 1,000 Hz. Adjust the output amplitude to 5 VPP.

Note the wave form. The wave form should look like the following picture.

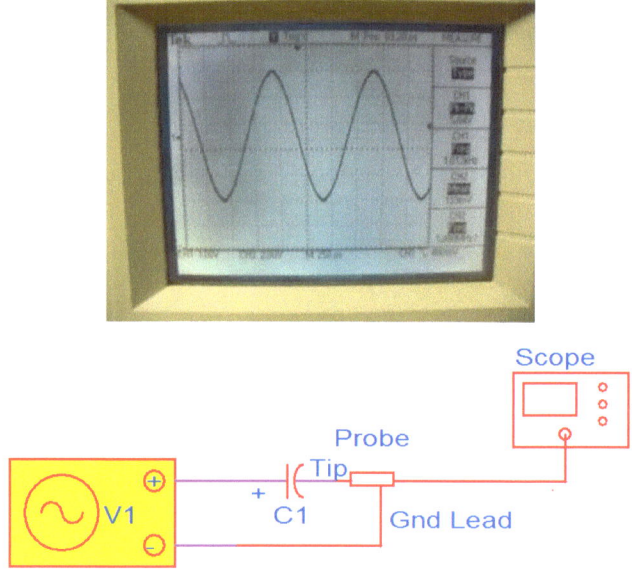

Figure 29 B

Now take the positive lead of a 1,000 µF Electrolytic Capacitor and connect to the generator positive output. Connect the scope probe to the capacitor negative lead, and the negative scope lead to the generator ground, as shown in Figure 29B. Note the wave form.

The wave form should be the same.

Lab 10

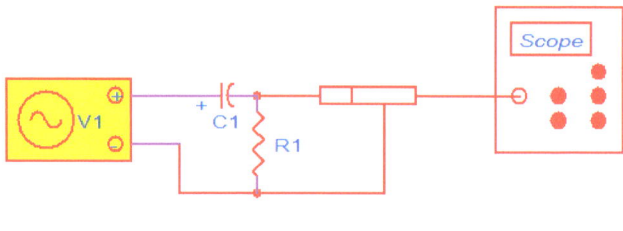

Figure 30

Note when doing any lab assignment be sure the power source is off while making connections.

Now let's take the same lab we did above with the 1,000 µF capacitor connected to the generator positive, and then take the 1,000 ohm resistor used in an earlier lab, connect to the negative side of the capacitor and the other end of the resistor to the negative side of the generator. Set the generator to 60 hertz and a level of 5 VPP. On the Scope set the volts/division or CH-1 to read 1 or 5 volts per unit. Set the sweep time/division or Horizontal to 5 milliseconds. Set the vertical position so the Line is in the center of the screen. Put the positive lead of the scope to the junction of the capacitor and resistor. Connect the negative lead of the scope to the generator negative.

Note when tying a capacitor and resistor together, you cannot figure the series voltage drop like two resistors in series, there are other factors that are involved. As I explained at the beginning of this book, we were not going to get into advance formulas, just the basic. Therefore, we will do the experiments and note the differences.

Question 3: Note the amplitude of the signal on the scope. _____

Now let's set up the same circuit but change the capacitor to a 1 UF.

Question 4: Note the amplitude of the signal on the scope _____ it will be reduced.

Now let's do the same lab as above with the 1,000 UF capacitor and set the generator to 1000 Hz. change the sweep time/division or Horizontal to 250 microseconds.

Question 5: Note the voltage level of the sine wave _____.

Now let's do the same lab as above with the 1 µf capacitor and set the generator set to 1000 Hz.

Question 6: Note the voltage level of the sine wave _____.

Now let's do a lab showing how a capacitor blocks dc.

Connect the positive side of a 1uF capacitor to the positive side of the 12 VDC power supply, connect the negative side of the capacitor to one side of a 1,000 (1K) resistor, note the color for the resistor is Brown, Black, Brown. Tie the opposite end of the resistor to the negative side of the power supply. Now tie the positive lead of the voltmeter to the connection point of the capacitor and resistor. Tie the negative side of the meter to the negative side of the power supply. Set the meter to DC volts.

Lab 12

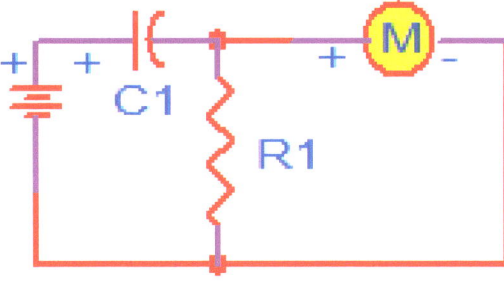

Figure 31

Note the voltage may start high because the charge of the capacitor, but it will go to 0 VDC and stay there.

Note when doing any lab assignment be sure the power source is off while making connections.

Now let's do a lab showing how a capacitor is used for power supply filtering.

Lab 13

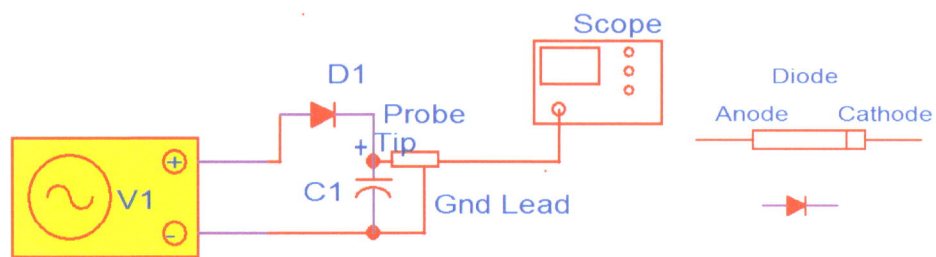

Figure 32

Note when doing any lab assignment be sure the power source is off while making connections.

Take a diode and connect the anode end to the positive side of your signal generator, set the generator to 60 HZ., 5 VPP. Note the anode end of the diode is the end opposite the stripe. Then connect the cathode to the positive lead of the 1,000 UF capacitor. Connect the negative end of the capacitor to the negative side of the generator. Now connect the positive side of the scope probe to the junction of the diode and capacitor and connect the negative side of the scope to the generator negative terminal. Set the scope to DC input. Note the signal. There is no sine wave just a DC voltage.

Question 7: What DC voltage do you get _____

This is a basic power supply filter circuit. A test generator does not give much power, if you were to use a power transformer, you would have some usable DC power. The only thing with this circuit is the voltage will change as you add a load. In a later chapter we will add circuitry to control the voltage at a constant value.

Answers to questions

Question 1: .3786 ohms

Question 2: .0003768 ohms

Question 3: Should be around 4.6 VPP

Question 4: Should be around 1.7 VPP. The level drops due to the increase in impedance with a lower value capacitor.

Question 5: Should be around 4.6 VPP

Question 6: Should be around 4.6 VPP. The level stayed the same because the increase in frequency has less loss in the lower value capacitor.

Question 7: Should be around 2.7 Volts DC with a straight line.

Chapter 8
Inductors and Transformers

Now let's talk about inductors and transformers. Inductors are used to filter high frequencies out and pass low frequencies. Transformers are used to step voltage up or down.

Inductors and transformers come in many sizes and shapes.

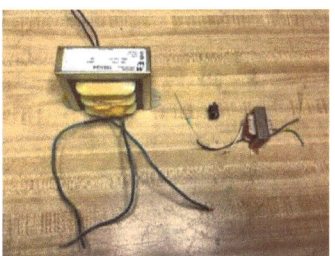

Figure 33A

Figure 33B

Figure 33C

The units of measure with inductors are. Inductance, measured in Henrys or micro-Henrys, impedance in ohms, frequency in hertz and amperage in amps. Note the impedance is in reference to AC voltage, but inductors also have DC resistance when passing DC voltage.

The formula for calculating the impedance, which is like resistance in resistors,

$XL = 2 \pi * F * L$ π Note this is Pi equal to 3.14, the F is frequency and L inductance.

Now let's use different frequencies and see how the inductor reacts with these frequencies.

Let's use a 10 mil Henry coil (.01 Henry), a 100 ohm resistor, and a frequency of 500 hertz, note the color for the resistor is Brown, Black, Brown.

Question 1: XL = 2*3.14 * 500 * .01 what the result is. _____

Now if we apply this in the following circuit, the resistor is being used as a load.

Now let's change the frequency to 50,000 hertz (50 K hertz) using the same formula

Question 2: XL = 2*3.14 * 50,000 * .01 what is the result. _____

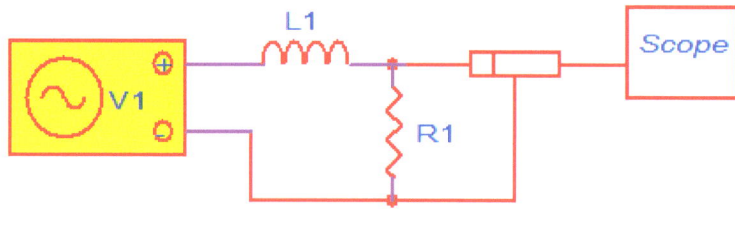

Figure 34

Note when doing any lab assignment be sure the power source is off while making connections.

Lab 14

Connect one end of the 10 ml henry inductor to the positive output of the test generator. Now tie the other end of the inductor to a 1000 ohm resistor, and the other end of the resistor to the Gnd. side of the generator. Connect the probe of a scope to the center point of the inductor and resistor. Tie the Gnd. side of the scope to the Gnd. side of the generator. Set the generator to 500 hertz and 5 VPP. On the Scope set the volts/division or CH-1 to read 1 volt per unit. Set the sweep time/division or Horizontal to 500 microseconds. Set the vertical position so the Line is in the center of the screen.

Note when tying an inductor and resistor together, you cannot figure the AC series voltage drop like two resistors in series, there are other factors that are involved. As I explained at the beginning of this book we were not going to get into advance formulas, just the basic. Therefore, we will do the experiments and note the differences.

Question 3: Note the signal level at the common point. _____

Now let's change the frequency of the generator to 50,000 hertz. On the Scope set the volts/division or CH-1 to read 200 millivolts per unit. Set the sweep time/division or Horizontal to 10 microseconds. Set the vertical position so the Line is in the center of the screen.

Question 4: What is the signal level now? _____

As you can see, the higher the frequency, the lower the level, due to the increase, in impedance.

Now let's talk about how an inductor passes DC voltage.

Note when doing any lab assignment be sure the power source is off while making connections.

Lab 15

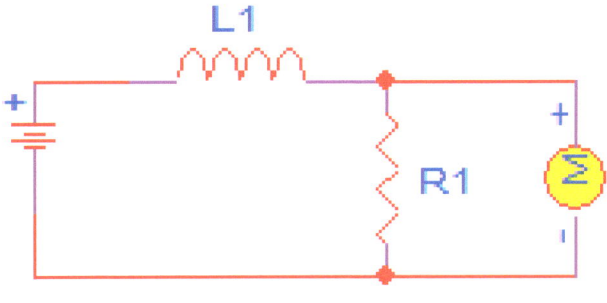

Figure 35

You connect the one end of the inductor to the positive lead of the 12 volt power supply, connect the other end of the inductor to a 1,000 ohm resistor, and connect the other end of the resistor to the negative side of the power supply. Connect the positive lead of your voltmeter to the center point of the inductor and resistor, and the negative lead to the negative side of the power supply.

Question 5: Note the voltage _____ this voltage should be the same as the power supply, this shows how an inductor passes DC voltage. Inductors do have a DC resistance to them as well as the ac impedance. Note when selecting an inductor, you select one that has the capability to handle the current you require to be passed.

Transformers: Transformers are used for AC voltage step down, for AC voltage step up, for isolating two circuits.

Transformers come in many shapes and sizes, including huge transformers used by the power companies.

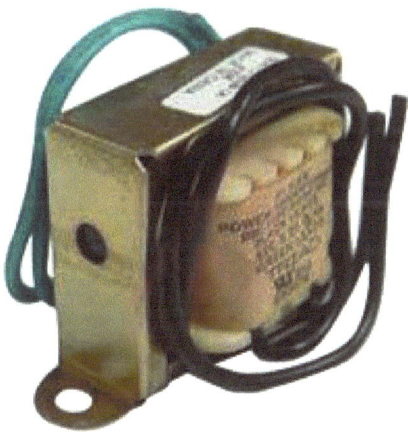

Figure 36

Transformers have many features, some have what is called center taps, some step voltage up some step voltage down, some have multiple windings allow for multiple voltage outputs.

Lets 1st talk about a transformer with a center tap. This is where you get half the voltage between either outside lead to the center point lead.

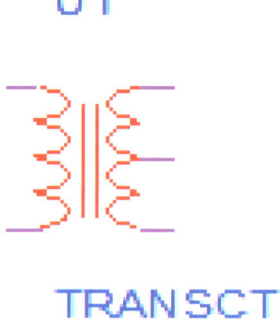

Figure 37

Now let's talk about a multi tap transformer. This allows for multiple voltage outputs at the same time and isolation from each output.

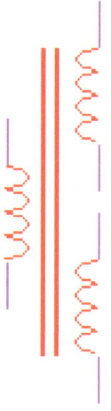

Figure 38

Now we will talk about step down and step up transformers. The following lab will show how this is accomplished.

Lab 16

Take the 120 VAC transformer listed in the appendix and connect one side of the input or labeled 120 VAC to the generator positive output, and the other input lead of the transformer to the Gnd. side of the generator. For setup purposes connect the scope probe to the positive side of the generator, and the negative side of the scope to the Gnd. Side of the generator. Set the generator to 60 Hertz; adjust the generator to measure 5 VPP. On the Scope set the volts/division or CH-1 to read 1 volt per unit. Set the sweep time/division or Horizontal to 5 milliseconds. Set the vertical position so the Line is in the center of the screen.

Lab 16

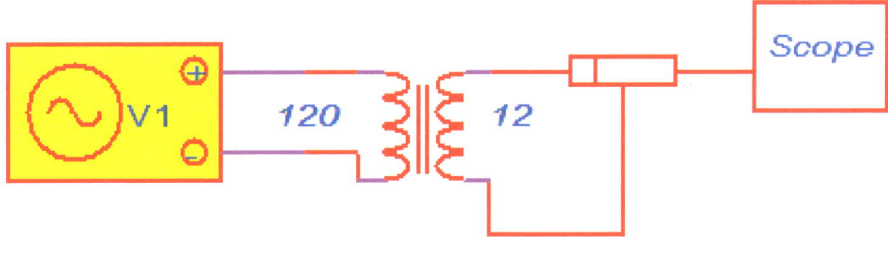

Figure 40

Note when doing any lab assignment be sure the power source is off while making connections.

Now move the scope probe to the output leads on the opposite side of the transformer may be labeled 12 VAC, connect the probe to one lead, then connect the other output lead of the transformer to the Gnd. side of the scope. On the Scope set the volts/division or CH-1 to read 100 millivolts per unit.

Question 6: Note the voltage reading on the scope _____, this value will be the fraction of the input 5 VPP. If we take the ratio of the 12 volt output to the 120 volt input it is 10 to 1. Therefore, your lab voltage should be around .5 volts 1/10 of the 5 volt generator. Note your reading may be higher or lower than .5 volts depending on the winding of the transformer.

Lab 17

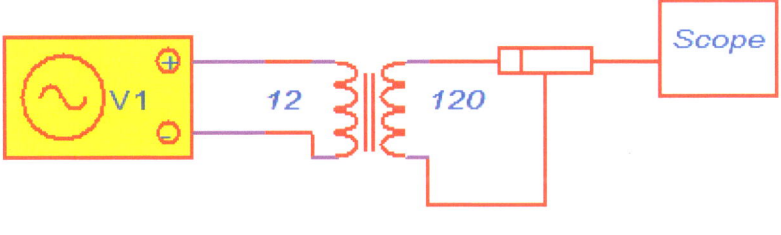

Figure 41

Note when doing any lab assignment be sure the power source is off while making connections.

Take the 120 VAC transformer listed in the appendix and connect one side of the output or labeled 12 VAC to the generator positive output, and the other output lead of the transformer to the Gnd. side of the generator. For setup purpose connect the scope probe to the positive side of the generator and the negative lead to the negative side of the generator, note the voltage level, set the volts/division or CH-1 to read 20 millivolts per unit. Now disconnect the scope from the 12 volt side of the transformer and connect on of the input leads on the side of the transformer may be labeled 120 VAC, connect the other input lead of the transformer to the Gnd. Side of the scope. On the Scope set the volts/division or CH-1 to read 100 millivolts per unit.

Question 7: Note the voltage reading on the scope _____, this value will be the multiple of the input voltage. If we take the ratio of the 12 volt output to the 120 volt input it is 10 to 1. Therefore you lab voltage should be 10 time the generator voltage.

Answers to questions

Question 1: 31.4 ohms

Question 2: 3,140 ohms Note by increasing the frequency you increase the resistance.

Question 3: Approximately 4.3 VPP

Question 4: Approximately 1.6 VPP. Note the increase in frequency reduces the level.

Question 5 : 12 VDC

Question 6 : .5 VPP

Question 7 : 5 VPP

Chapter 9
Other Signals

RF radio frequency signals. These are AC signals with a modulated either Analog, or digital signal riding on it. This is what AM radio, FM radio, Television, Cellular phones, remote controls and many other wireless communications. I am not going into detail in this book on this subject, but I thought you should be aware of these signals.

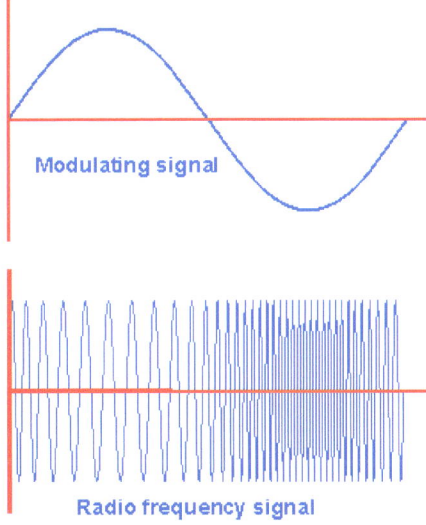

Digital signal: This is the main type of control signals for controlling manufacturing equipment, computers, cars, and many electronic devices. There are a lot of misconceptions of what a digital signal is compared to an analog signal. A standard wall switch is a digital device. A digital device is one that is either on (1) or off (0). An analog device is one that varies in level, such as conventional volume control. All speakers, microphones, TV camera pickup devices and TV screens are analog devices. If a speaker was only capable of digital, you would hear full volume or no sound. With analog you hear varying sound levels. I am not going into detail in this book on this subject, but I thought you should be aware of these signals.

Digital signal:

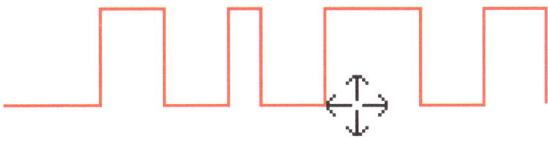

RF signals are read with a field strength meter. We will not do a lab on this because the cost for a field strength meter can be expensive. Field strength meters read Db for signal strength and frequency or channels to determine whether they are on the right frequency. Many things affect RF signals, cable loss, feeding through devices, poor connections and improper end of line termination.

Weak analog RF signals can cause snow in analog video or noise in audio. Weak digital signals will cause artifacts and freezing of the image in the picture or sound, note this is true with digital signals as well as analog signals.

Over amplified signals will have noise in sound or lines in a TV image.

Improper connections of RF signals will cause weak signals, interference and emission beyond the cabling system.

RF signals can be split in many directions using one of the following, splitter, and taps. When using a splitter all end of lines need to be terminated, or ghosting can occur. Taps are isolated devices, it is still recommended for end of line termination, but it is not as critical with a tap.

Splitters are typically used for feeding trunk lines, and taps are used for feeding individual devices such as TV's.

Chapter 10
Diodes

Diodes come in several shapes, sizes and types. Led is a form of a diode. Light Emitting Diode:

Diodes

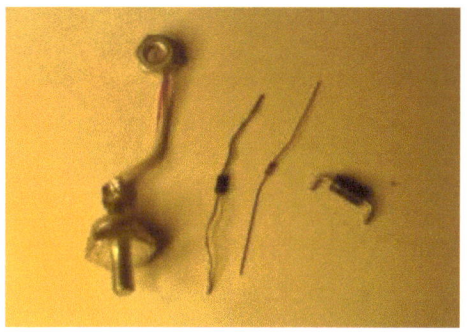

Led's

Diodes are used in many applications. The following are some of the functions of diodes. Standard diodes AC to DC conversion, directional control, Zener diodes are used for voltage control; LED's are used for indicators, and many other uses.

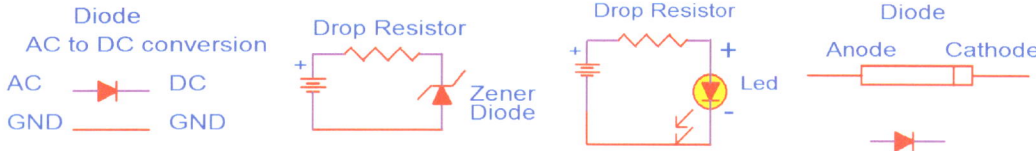

Figure 42

AC to DC conversion Lab 18

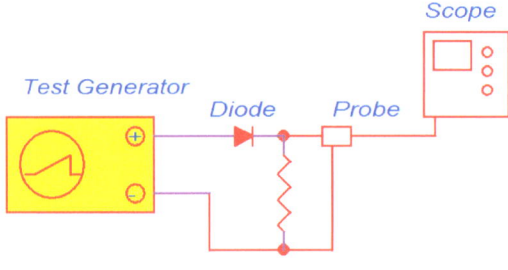

Figure 43

Note when doing any lab assignment be sure the power source is off while making connections.

Take a diode and connect the anode end to the positive side of your signal generator. Note the anode end of the diode is the end opposite the stripe. Connect a 390 ohm resistor from the cathode side of the diode to the negative side of the generator. Connect the Scope probe to the junction of the diode and resistor. Now connect the cathode side of the diode to the positive side of the generator and connect the negative side of the scope to the generator negative terminal. Set the generator to 500 hertz and 5 VPP. On the Scope set the volts/division or CH-1 to read 1 volt per unit. Set the sweep time/division or Horizontal to 500 microseconds. Set the vertical position so the Line is in the center of the screen. Reference figure 43

Note the signal the bottom half of the sine wave is gone, that is because only the positive portion of the signal passes through the diode in this configuration.

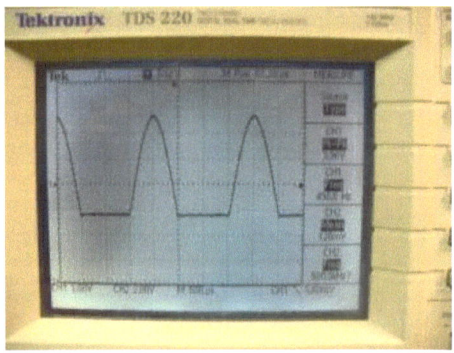

Figure 44

Lab 19

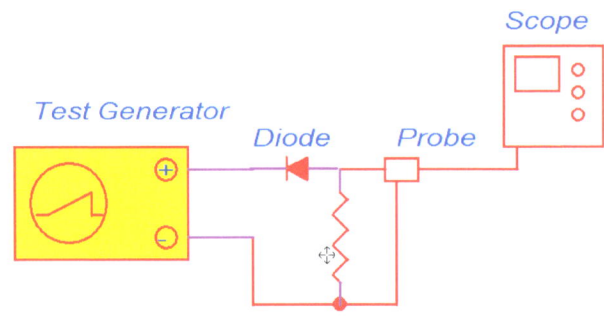

Figure 45

Now connect the cathode end of the diode to the test generator positive post. Note the anode end of the diode is the end opposite the stripe. Connect a 390 ohm resistor from the anode side of the diode to the negative side of the generator. Connect the Scope probe to the positive side of the generator and connect the negative side of the scope to the generator negative terminal. Set the generator to 500 hertz and 5 VPP. On the Scope set the volts/division or CH-1 to read 1 volt per unit. Set the sweep time/division or Horizontal to 500 microseconds. Set the vertical position so the Line is in the center of the screen. Reference figure 43

Note the signal, it will only pass the negative portion of the sine wave. This is because only the negative signal passes in reverse.

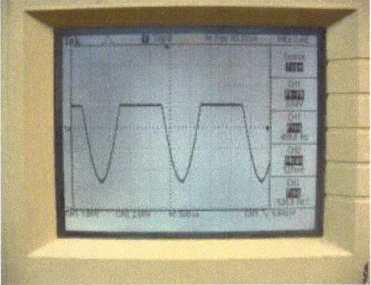

Figure 46

Voltage control Lab 20

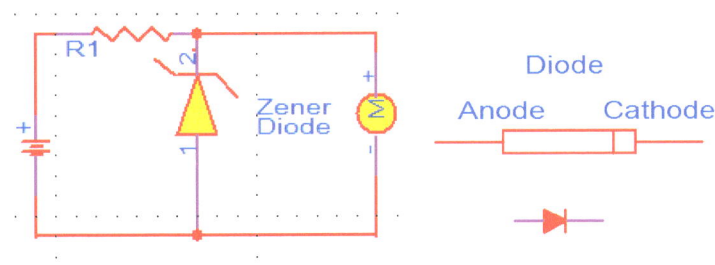

Figure 47

Note when doing any lab assignment be sure the power source is off while making connections.

A Zener diode is used to control voltage.

Lab, connect the one end of A 120 ohm ½ watt resistor to the positive post of a 12 VDC power source, connect the other end of the resistor to the cathode end of A 1N4735A Zener diode with the White band. Connect the Anode end of the diode to the negative side of the power supply. Connect the positive lead of the meter to the connecting point of the Zener diode and resistor. Connect the negative lead of the meter to the power supply negative.

Question 1: What voltage do you get _____

LED indicator Lab 21

A led is a form of a diode, therefor the direction is critical. Also, LED's are a voltage limited device, so you need a resistor in series with the LED

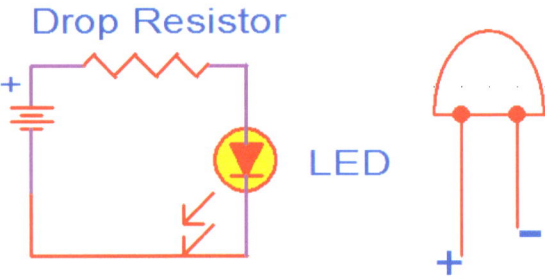

Figure 48

Note when doing any lab assignment be sure the power source is off while making connections.

Note the Led picture. The longer lead is the positive lead Anode, and the shorter lead is the Cathode negative lead.

Lab connect the one end of A 390 Ohm ½ watt resistor to the positive post of a 12 VDC power source, connect the other end of the resistor to the anode end of A led, connect the cathode side of the led to the negative side of the power supply. Note the resistor value is based on a 2 volt 30 ma (.03 amp) Led. If you use a different voltage LED you may need to use the formula R=E/I and the E would be the difference of the LED voltage and the 12 volt power supply, and the I would be the current rating of the LED. The LED should light normal brightness.

Now let's change the resistor to A 12K (12,000) Ohm 1/4 watt resistor to the positive post of a 12 VDC power source, connect the other end of resistor to the anode end of A led, connect the cathode side of the led to the negative side of the power supply. The LED should be lit but dimmer.

Answers to questions

Question 1: 6.2 Volts DC

Chapter 11
Switches

Figure 50

Switches come in many shapes and sizes. They can be simple light switches, toggle switches, push button switches, slide switches, rotary switches and rocker switches.

Switches are rated for both AC and DC voltage and Current. Some switches give an amount of actuation uses, before failing. A switch is a digital device since it is either on or off. Switches can be single pole single throw SPST, single pole double throw SPDT, and many other configurations. An example of a SPDT switch is for controlling light from two different locations.

Labs using a SPDT switch:

Lab 22

Note when doing any lab assignment be sure the power source is off while making connections.

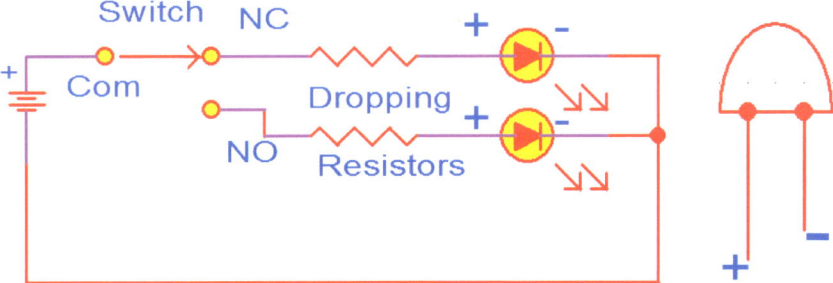

Figure 51

Note the Led picture. The longer lead is the positive lead Anode, and the shorter lead is the Cathode negative lead.

Connect the positive side of the 12 VDC power source to the switch Com, connect the NC contact to one end of a 390 ohm ½ watt resistor connect the other end of the resistor to the anode end of a Led, connect the Cathode side of the LED to the negative side of the power supply. Now connect the NO contact to one end of a 390-ohm ½ watt resistor, connect the other end of the resistor to the anode end of a Led, now connect the Cathode side of the LED to the negative side of the power supply.

When you toggle the switch back and forth one or the other LED will work.

Lab two-way light switch Lab 23

Note when doing any lab assignment be sure the power source is off while making connections.

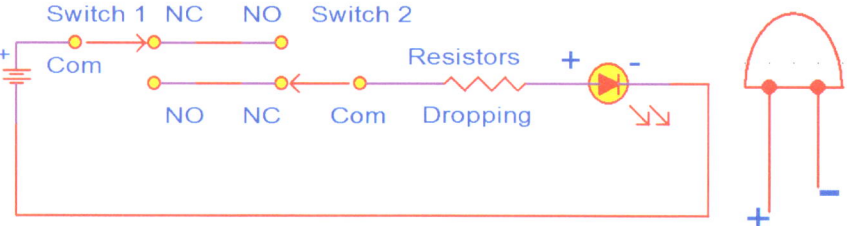

Figure 52

Note the Led picture. The longer lead is the positive lead Anode, and the shorter lead is the Cathode negative lead.

Connect the positive side of the 12-volt power source to Switch 1 Com, tie Switch 1 NC contact to Switch 2 NO contact, and then tie Switch 1 NO contact to Switch 2 NC contact. Tie Switch 2 Com to 390 ohm ½ watt resistor, tie the other end of the resistor to the Anode side of the LED, and tie the Cathode side of the LED to the negative side of the power source.

Now when you Turn switch 1 on and switch 2 off the LED lights when you turn Switch 1 off and Switch 2 on the LED lights, but when you have the wrong combination, the LED will be off.

This simulates a two-way light switch used typically for stair lighting with a switch at the top and bottom of the stairs. The only difference you would be working with 120VAC and no resistors, and a light bulb instead a LED.

Chapter 12
Relays and Solenoids

Figure 53

Relays come in all different shapes and sizes including some very large relays for High power system.

Relays are used for High voltage, High current, time control, and some relays have multiple contacts allowing controlling multiple voltages.

Relays consist of a coil and one or more pairs of contacts. The coils can be DC rated, or AC rated. The contracts will have both voltage, current, AC and DC ratings. Note the DC and AC current and voltage ratings may be different. Contacts can be Normally Open (NO), Normally Closed (NC), and common (C). A single contact relay may be listed as A Single Pole Single Throw (SPST). If a relay has multiple contacts, they may be listed as Single Pole Double Throw (SPDT) as well as other configurations.

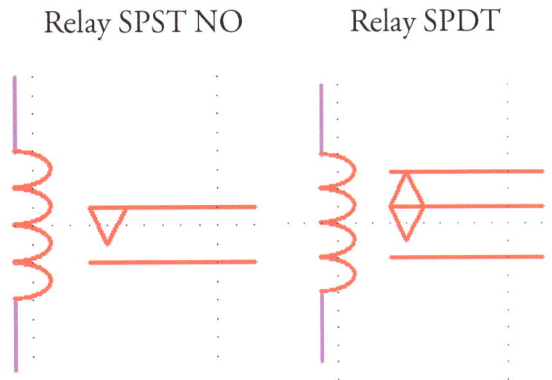

Figure 54

Example of a relay use: You have a large AC motor to turn on and off. It would require a large cable between the switch and the motor. Using a relay will allow a small switch and smaller cable to be located anywhere within a reasonable distance. This drawing is using a 24 VAC relay or could be a 24 VDC relay.

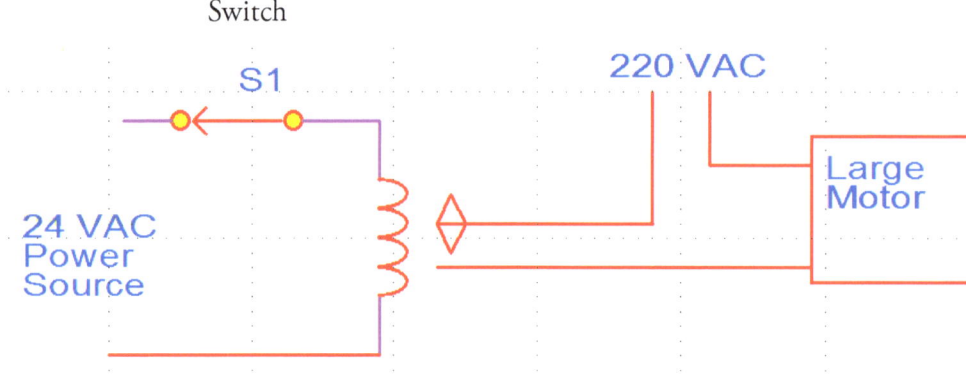

Figure 55

Lab 24

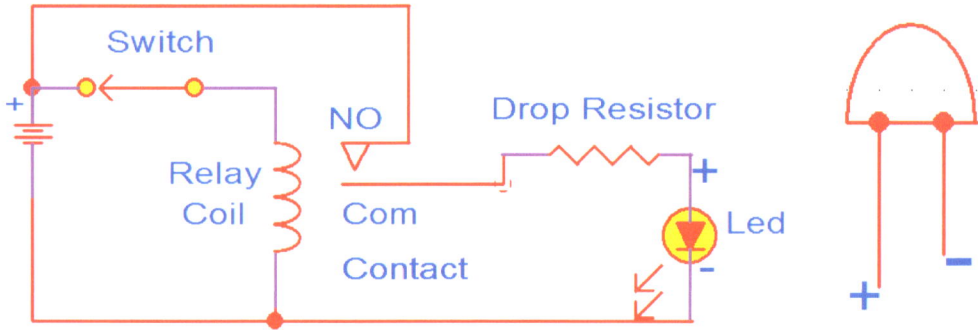

Figure 56

Note when doing any lab assignment be sure the power source is off while making connections.

Note the Led picture. The longer lead is the positive lead Anode, and the shorter lead is the Cathode negative lead.

You can use a relay with a screw terminal socket or a printed circuit version of the relay. The relay pin out should be stamped on the relay, if not go to the manufactures Web page for detail. Note if you use the printed circuit relay, be sure to straddle the cut in the center of the prototype board.

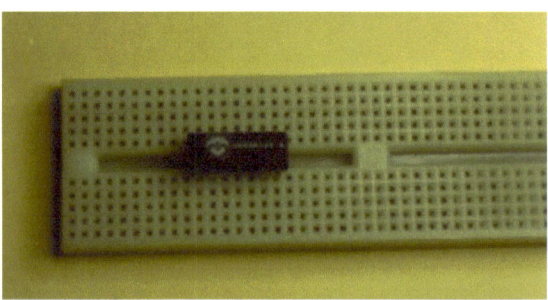

Figure 57

Connect the positive side of the 12 VDC power source to one side of a switch, then connect the other side of the switch to one side of the relay coil. Connect the other side of the relay coil to the negative side of the power source. Connect the positive side of the power source to the common contact of the relay. Connect the normally open contact to a 390 ohm ½ watt resistor. Connect the other end of the resistor to the anode side of the led. Connecting the cathode side of the led to the negative side of the power source. Now when you turn the switch on and off it will turn the led on and off.

Solenoids:

Solenoids are used to push or pull mechanical devices.

Figure 58

Lab 25

Note when doing any lab assignment be sure the power source is off while making connections.

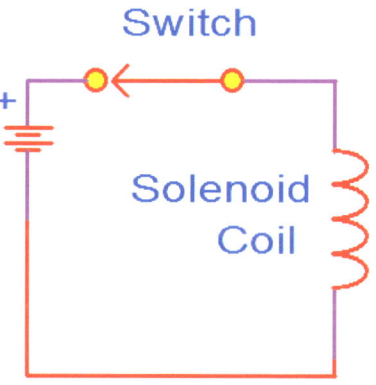

Figure 59

Connect the positive side of the 12 VDC power source to one side of the switch, connect the other side of the switch to the positive side of the solenoid, and connect the negative side of the solenoid to the negative side of the power supply. Note if you use an AC relay you will need an AC power source.

When the switch is turned on and off the plunger of the solenoid goes in and out.

Chapter 13
Transistors

Figure 60

Transistors come in all shapes and sizes. Transistors can be low power or high power. Standard transistors are listed as NPN, or PNP. JFET transistors come as N channel or P channel. Other types of transistors are UJT and Darlington Pair. Also, IC chips consist of large amounts of transistors and diodes.

Transistors have several uses. They can act as switches, amplifiers, voltage control, current control and many other uses.

Let's talk about a standard NPN transistor. This transistor has a Base used typically as the input, an Emitter used as the drain and a Collector which controls the output.

Lab 26: Use of an NPN transistor: This lab shows how a low voltage of .6 - .8 volts at the base can control a 12 volt relay. When used with an audio or other form of AC input signal this would allow amplifying the signal.

Note when doing any lab assignment be sure the power source is off while making connections.

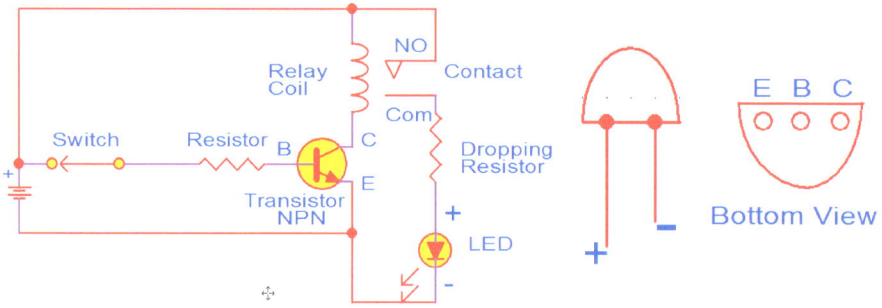

Leads pointing at you Figure 61   LED   Transistor

Note the Led picture. The longer lead is the positive lead Anode, and the shorter lead is the Cathode negative lead.

Note the transistor picture showing the bottom view of the transistor with the leads pointing at you. Note be sure to hook the transistor up correctly, if not hooked up correctly this part can be damaged easily. The emitter (E) is on the left, the base (B) is in the center, and the collector (C) is on the right. Transistors come with several mounting and lead configurations.

Connect the positive side of the 12VDC power to one side of the switch, connect the other side of the switch to A 12,000-ohm resistor (12K) ¼ watt, connect the other side of the resistor to the base (B) of the transistor, connect the emitter (E) of the transistor to the negative side of the power supply. Connect one side of the relay coil to the positive side of the power supply; connect the other side of the relay coil to the collector (C) of the transistor. Connect the NO contact of the relay to the positive side of the power supply, connect the relay Common to A 390-ohm ½ watt resistor. Connect the other side of this resistor to the anode side of the LED. Connect the cathode side of the LED to the negative side of the power supply.

When turning the switch on and off it will turn the relay on and off. This will then turn the LED on and off.

Now take your voltmeter, connect the positive lead to the base (B) of the transistor, and connect the negative lead to the negative side of the power supply.

Transistors are typically in between a switch or other control device and IC chips.

Question 1: Note the voltage _____.

Answers to questions

Question 1: This value should be around .6 to .8 volts. This shows how a transistor will allow a low voltage to control a much higher voltage. As you saw how a low voltage can control a larger voltage, this is the same theory of taking a low audio level and creating a much higher audio output, this is known as amplification.

Chapter 14
Audio

Audio systems have inputs and outputs. Audio is usually measured in db. (Decibels) And has frequency ranges of 20 Hz to 20,000 Hz. As you get older the higher frequencies tend to be weaker.

Inputs can include devices, such as microphones, CD players, Tuners, and many forms of digital devices.

Output includes speakers, recording devices and feeds to other systems.

Note all input devices and output devices are always analog, however in between many devices today use digital with analog to digital processors for incoming and digital to analog processors for speakers.

Comparison of Analog and Digital:

Analog has been around a long time, and analog is the purest sound available, however when recording audio or sending audio long distances, multiple generations can cause degradation of the sound. Digital audio has many parameters. Digital audio can be reproduced over and over with very little degradation. Digital audio, however, is compressed and depending on the bit format will determine the sound quality. Example children's toys typically sound tiny, as CD and other high-end devices sound much clearer.

Input devises:

Hand microphone

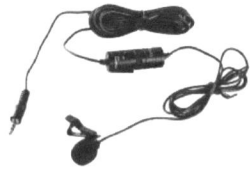

Lavallière microphone

Figure 62

Microphones are analog input devices with normally low levels such as -40 to -60 db. , may have impedances ranging from 250 ohms to 5 K ohms. Microphone elements can be tied directly to amplifier inputs or may have a preamp built in the microphone; these microphones are called condenser microphones and require a phantom voltage.

All other analog inputs can vary in levels of -20 to +10 db., may have an impedance of 250 ohms to 10 K ohms.

Unbalanced audio runs are vulnerable of interference and should be short. Balanced inputs can go long distance and are less vulnerable of interference. An example of an unbalanced connection is a RCA plug that has a center pin and outer shield. An example of a balanced connection would be an XLR plug that has 3 pins, Hi, Lo and Gnd.

<u>Output devices:</u>

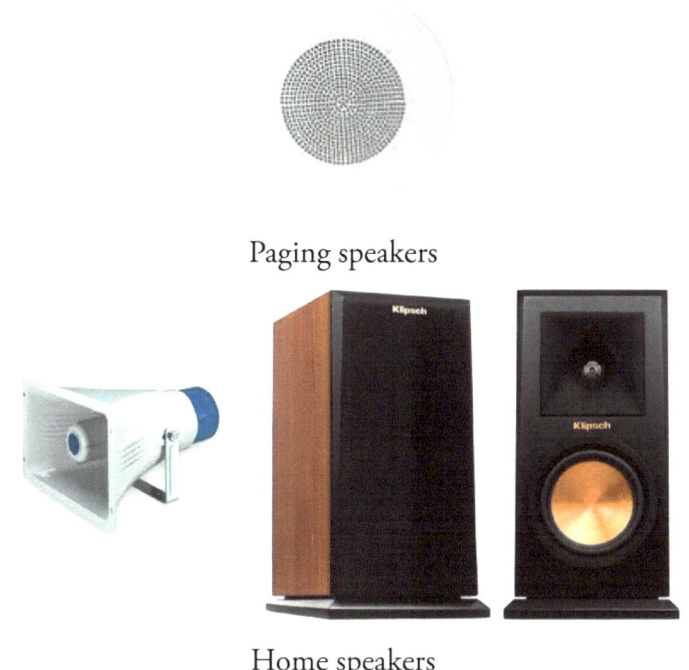

Paging speakers

Home speakers

Figure 63

Speakers:

There are basically four speaker formats. Speakers have both AC resistance known as impedance and DC resistance.

<u>Direct</u>, these have impedances of 4-16 ohm; these are your standard home, car and pro sound speakers. Caution must be taken when connecting multiple speakers of this type across an amplifier, some amps have output impedance of 2-8 ohms. Example you have two 8 ohm speakers you want to parallel, the resulting impedance is 4 ohms, most home amps are designed for 8 ohms, therefore you would overload the amplifier and could damage the amplifier.

<u>Constant Voltage</u>, these speakers are listed by voltage ratings, these come 25 volt, 70 volt, or 100 volt, these speakers are used for paging in places like stores, restaurants, schools, hospitals and many more application's. These speakers have taps which allow a different level per speaker or speaker groups. Example in a school, the halls typically are set at either ½ watt or 1 watt, but the gym or auditorium may be set at 10 or 15 watts. These

types of speakers use matching transformers that convert the 25 volt or 70 level line to typically 8 ohms of the speaker. The actual impedance of these devices is higher, therefore multiple speakers can be parallel without overloading the amplifier.

Matching transformer:

Figure 64

Cable size in reference to speakers: We talked about cable size in the resistance chapter, this also relates to speakers. For example, direct 8 ohm speakers being used in an auditorium. It is important to use heavy enough wire depending on cable length. Also with 70 volt distributed sound systems, as you increase the amount of speakers, and length of a run the cable size also will become critical.

Amplified speakers, these are typically used with computers. These speakers have an amplifier input built into them; therefore they can be hooked to a line level output such as a headphone jack on a device. Amplified speakers can also come with digital input with a built-in processor to change the audio to analog for the actual speaker.

Figure 65

Digital Speakers: These speakers are used with pro sound systems. These speakers require AC power at the speaker plus a digital audio feed from the sound system. These speakers are quite expensive, but do not require power amplifiers, or large audio cable feeding them. These are used typically in large auditoriums.

Recording devices:

These devices come in various types and configurations. Analog type devices typically have either unbalanced or balanced inputs. Unbalanced inputs have only two style connections, such as a RCA plug or a 3.5 MM two conductor plug. Balanced inputs use three conductor plugs like XLR plugs. Unbalanced audio runs are vulnerable of interference and should be short. Balanced inputs can go long distance and are less vulnerable of interference.

Sending audio to other systems:

Can be challenging, you must deal with audio loss, interference and 60 Hz hum. With analog it is recommended using balance audio and only connects the shield at the input side of the system. If you are feeding several systems, it is recommended to use an Audio Distribution Amplifier. Also, cable loss is critical for long distances. With digital signals converted to data, digital systems have cable limitations of typically 100 meters, on copper, but with fiber you can get distances up to several miles.

Lab

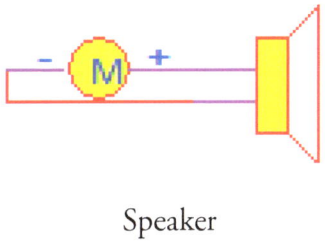

Speaker

Figure 66

Connect the positive side of your meter to one of the speaker connections, next tie the negative side of the meter to the other speaker connection. Set the meter to the lowest ohms scale.

Question 1: Note the impedance value listed on the speaker.

Question 2: Note the meter reading _____

Answers to questions

Question 1: The speaker impedance rating should be listed like 8 ohms.

Question 2: This value should be less than the listed speaker impedance; this is because a meter reads the DC resistance not impedance. Therefor speakers cannot be read with an ohm meter, you use what is called an impedance meter. An impedance meter reads the AC resistance of the speaker or transformer, typically the impedance meter will come with a chart to calculate the loading of an amplifier in Watts. These are used typically with large sound and paging systems to make sure you do not overload the amplifier.

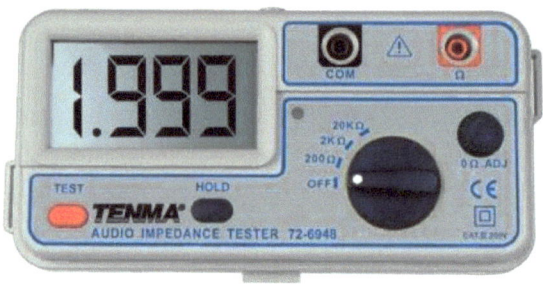

Figure 67

Chapter 15
Trouble Shooting

Trouble shooting is one of the most important parts of working with electronics.

Your most common tool for trouble shooting is the volt ohm meter. Be sure on how to use your meter. Other tools to test with may be an oscilloscope, a field strength meter, and a test generator.

With the power off check all connections. Sometimes when screwing terminals down you might miss one. Also be sure to use the proper size and type tool for making terminations. If the wrong crimping tool is used, you may get an intermittent connection. Check all solder joints visually, be sure there are no cold solder joints, a cold solder joint is normally has a crack around the joint.

The first place to start trouble shooting is starting with the power source, be sure you have proper power coming from the power source, some power supplies have multiple outputs, be sure all outputs are working correctly.

Next check for continuity. Using your meter follow the path. Typically, you should be able to read voltage through the complete path. Be sure to be on the right type of voltage function on the meter, such as AC or DC. If working with audio circuits, you will need a test tone generator to supply signal through the path, and an oscilloscope to read the signal. If you are working with high frequencies such as TV or Radio signals, you will need a field strength meter or a spectrum analyzer.

If you are working with a shorted or open circuit. With the power off 1st read continuity at your end point using the ohms scale, on the multifunction meter. Then continue taking measurements, working your way back towards the source of power or signal.

Systems such as sound and fire alarm can be sensitive to grounding on field wiring. The best way to test this is to shut all power off. Connect the negative side of the meter to earth ground, then take the probe and check each field cable. Be sure the meter is set on 10,000 ohms scale and should show no measurement.

Appendix

<u>Suppliers of electronic test equipment and materials</u>: Note this is just a parcel list I work with. There are many more suppliers.

Allied Electronics

Digi-key Electronics

Jameco Electronics

Mouser Electronics

Newark/MCM Electronics

Amazon

<u>Lab systems</u>

There are many manufactures of lab systems.

<u>Factory Built Lab unit.</u>   Jameco 1919211 Digital/Analog Test Laboratory

Or

<u>Build your own Lab unit. Note this package will consist of several parts, and parts models may change.</u>

Jameco 2244113 or equal proto type board with wire jumpers

Newark 79X4272 or equivalent variable voltage power supply, with a range of 1 to at least 12 volts and capable of at least 1 amp. Note this power supply can have higher voltage and higher amperage capability.

Newark 66F3575 or equal test signal generator with a frequency range of at least 20 Hz to 100 K Hz. This unit has both sinewave and square wave outputs. Note the signal generator can have a wider range of frequencies beyond the 100 K Hz.

<u>Test Equipment needed</u>

The best supplier for test equipment is Newark Electronics, but other listed suppliers can also supply these materials.

Multipurpose volt meter example   Newark Electronics   72-7770

Oscilloscope	Newark Electronics	$300.00 to $400.00
Or		
Computer scope adapter	Newark Electronics	18X282

<u>Recommended materials for Labs</u>.

Note these materials can be bought from any of the above listed suppliers, depending on your future plans of electronics, you can purchase resistor and capacitor kits with multiple values including the ones needed for the experiments. Also, the individual pricing of these parts is low so you may want duplicates of like the transistor. I have listed parts number from Jameco.

(1) 1k ohm ¼ watt resistor	Jameco 690865
(1) 100 ohm ¼ watt resistor	Jameco 690620
(1) 2.2k ohm ¼ watt resistor	Jameco 690945
(1) 120 ohm ½ watt resistor	Jameco 690646
(2) 390 ohm ½ watt resistor	Jameco 690769
(1) 12,000 ohm ¼ watt resistor	Jameco 690881
(1) 1000µf 25 volt capacitor	Jameco 158298
(1) 1µf 50 volt capacitor	Jameco 94161
(1) 10 mill or 10,000micro Henry Inductor	Jameco 64271
(1) 1N4001 diode	Jameco 35975
(1) 1N4735A 6.2 Volt Zener diode	Jameco 36126
(2) LED 2.8 volt 30 ma	Jameco 697522
(1) 12 volt DC solenoid	Jameco 1919203
(2) SPDT toggle switch	Jameco 317236
(1) 12 volt DC Relay and socket, or a 12 volt DC relay Printed Circuit style.	Jameco 187258
(1) 2N3904 Transistor	Jameco 38359
(1) 120 to 12.6 volt transformer Note any transformer in this range.	Jameco 221356

Wire chart:

AWG	Diameter [inches]	Diameter [mm]	Area [mm²]	Resistance [Ohms / 1000 ft]	Resistance [Ohms / km]	Max Current [Amperes]	Max Frequency for 100% skin depth
0000 (4/0)	0.46	11.684	107	0.049	0.16072	302	125 Hz
000 (3/0)	0.4096	10.40384	85	0.0618	0.202704	239	160 Hz
00 (2/0)	0.3648	9.26592	67.4	0.0779	0.255512	190	200 Hz
0 (1/0)	0.3249	8.25246	53.5	0.0983	0.322424	150	250 Hz
1	0.2893	7.34822	42.4	0.1239	0.406392	119	325 Hz
2	0.2576	6.54304	33.6	0.1563	0.512664	94	410 Hz
3	0.2294	5.82676	26.7	0.197	0.64616	75	500 Hz
4	0.2043	5.18922	21.2	0.2485	0.81508	60	650 Hz
5	0.1819	4.62026	16.8	0.3133	1.027624	47	810 Hz
6	0.162	4.1148	13.3	0.3951	1.295928	37	1100 Hz
7	0.1443	3.66522	10.5	0.4982	1.634096	30	1300 Hz
8	0.1285	3.2639	8.37	0.6282	2.060496	24	1650 Hz
9	0.1144	2.90576	6.63	0.7921	2.598088	19	2050 Hz
10	0.1019	2.58826	5.26	0.9989	3.276392	15	2600 Hz
11	0.0907	2.30378	4.17	1.26	4.1328	12	3200 Hz
12	0.0808	2.05232	3.31	1.588	5.20864	9.3	4150 Hz
13	0.072	1.8288	2.62	2.003	6.56984	7.4	5300 Hz
14	0.0641	1.62814	2.08	2.525	8.282	5.9	6700 Hz
15	0.0571	1.45034	1.65	3.184	10.44352	4.7	8250 Hz
16	0.0508	1.29032	1.31	4.016	13.17248	3.7	11 k Hz
17	0.0453	1.15062	1.04	5.064	16.60992	2.9	13 k Hz
18	0.0403	1.02362	0.823	6.385	20.9428	2.3	17 kHz
19	0.0359	0.91186	0.653	8.051	26.40728	1.8	21 kHz
20	0.032	0.8128	0.518	10.15	33.292	1.5	27 kHz
21	0.0285	0.7239	0.41	12.8	41.984	1.2	33 kHz
22	0.0254	0.64516	0.326	16.14	52.9392	0.92	42 kHz
23	0.0226	0.57404	0.258	20.36	66.7808	0.729	53 kHz
24	0.0201	0.51054	0.205	25.67	84.1976	0.577	68 kHz

www.ingramcontent.com/pod-product-compliance
Lightning Source LLC
Chambersburg PA
CBHW040949050426
42337CB00049B/21